BLUE MOUNTAIN LAKE POEMS

Charles Bachman

with watercolors by Ann C. Colley

Order this book online at www.trafford.com
or email orders@trafford.com

Most Trafford titles are also available at major online book retailers.

Cover and layout design by Anno Domini Graphix

Printed in the United States of America.

ISBN: 978-1-4269-6228-8

Library of Congress Control Number: 2011906228

Trafford rev. 06/24/2011

 www.trafford.com

North America & international

toll-free: 1 888 232 4444 (USA & Canada)
phone: 250 383 6864 ✦ fax: 812 355 4082

Also by Charles Bachman

If Ariel Danced on the Moon, 2006
The Strange Lives of Mr. Shakovo, 2008
A Marked Peculiarity, 2009

www.charlesbachman.com

FOR NANCY

Thanks to three cherished colleagues and friends,

Ann C. Colley, who painted the wonderful watercolors for the cover and contents,
Jennifer Ryan, for support and fine introductions to my readings,
Stan Friesen, for the strikingly apt and imaginative cover designs for all of my books.

Pat Benton, for warm, comforting hospitality,
Nancy Townsend—brilliant musician, astute critic of my work, and the love of my life.

For quite a few years my wife Nancy and I have been making our annual fall visits to the Adirondacks, to hike, climb modest mountains, soak up the vivid autumn colors and other beautiful things, and enjoy the fellowship not only of our long-standing friends Jane, Tovey, and Richard, but also others we have grown close to over the years. While we have developed a special fondness for our base – the Hedges of Blue Mountain Lake – the beauty of all the places we visit here grows and grows on us. I hope these poems convey some of the awe, wonder, and love we feel for this very special "spot of earth."

Charles Bachman
North Tonawanda, NY
2011

CONTENTS

Dawn on Blue Mountain Lake

A long translucent cloud
scrims the far shoreline
into a wavering phantom
that rises to partly haze
the fall-leaved forest
carpeting the mountain.

Soft, cool breath
nudges the long ghost
into small puffs of smoke
that dance over the ripples
like wisps of elfin mist
into their own gentle demise.

The Loons are Calling

Especially in night's clearness
  or the cool bunched fog
    of dawn comes the full
      repertoire of chant
        from the faroff throat of the loon:

Rise, curve, descent—like thinner
  howl of wolf—level-pitch flutter,
    quick vocal nuances,
      all swept into the fullness
      of loon's cry.

As we take our last look,
  last listen for one more
    year, and as I go
      through the other part
      of my life out there:

During the bearded frost of winter
  I pause here and there to listen
    to something calling, calling
      in silent moments through
        the fine sproutings of spring,

warm amplitude of summer,
    as fall approaches more urgently
        it sings to the deep ear of my mind,
        as the eye of my heart opens
        to see it all again—

the loons beckon, beckon
    me back to the wood lodge,
        the lake, mountain, through all
        the dawns and crystal nights,
          with the fluted drift of their call.

Oddity

Why, one may ask, and how
did this strange loon creature
come to be?

Shaped for water like a feathered
dolphin who has suddenly grown
acute-angled legs, feet, extended
neck with point-beaked head,

head in stillness like a painted wood
carving of a head, yodel like laughter
that is anything but laughter, wail
a higher, prolonged wolf-like sound.

A seeming congeries of imitations and
analogies, nesting on land, barely
able to maneuver on land, primeval
anomaly of many aspects, why?

Ah, there is one now, its webbed feet
slap-pedalling the surface of Blue Mountain Lake
as it accelerates into its almost
impossible takeoff,

finally rising: angled image
almost invisible against the darkening
grey-green of the mountain then ah
silhouetted in startling piercing

through dusky sky under a horned moon.
Once more I breathe in, sigh,
not dreaming of asking why.

Rising out of

Even out of a night filled
with frog cricket cacophanies
the whohoowee of the loon's voice
wings itself above the trees.

Once a Prima Ballerina

Despite the steady sag
of her now-dragging
tutu of scanty branches,

she stiffens to maintain
a focussed dignity
of steady gaze,

regal straight-necked spine
from when, for all
too short a time,

she entranced her audience
of awe-struck creatures
and peers of green-decked pine.

Loon and Little One

Floating oval of solidness
in a bold embroidery of squarish
and round-dotted white
lichen, with a smaller arroyo

on the rear enlivened by
its resting passenger:
downy-brown baby bird,
its open beak and vital eyes
taking in all stern-wise

as our eyes move to the necklace:
a ring painting of shells
nestled against the crafted,
bold figurehead of the prow

whose jutting beak heads
into the morning wind,
guided by the strangely opaque
spark of a wide-open crimson eye.

Loon at Slumber

Small low hill floating isle
    of striking black and white
        striated, striped, spotted feathers
            nuzzled into by dark primal beaked

head, eyes invisible as she dreams
    of clear depths filled with swimming
        prey and white-mottled brown eggs
            in nest far from raccoon, gull, or turtle.

Loon at Dawn

In the glimpse of time
　　between shore-foothill cloud
　　　and thinning mist

its long wail
　　shatters the shroud
　　　of darkness.

Loon Pleasure-Diving

Still in its posture:
hieratic image
of a compact feathered
ship of roundish shape,
sculpted head, brow, and beak,

it moves as if by unseen
powers beyond itself,
then in an eye blink
becomes invisible
leaving scarcely the trace
of a ripple on the lake's face.

Brave Defender

Framed by the lake
looms an old maple
nearly severed by a split
about twenty feet up,
cradled, in typical fashion,
by neighboring saplings,
older trees.

It still hangs on
not by much
to its trunk stem's
still fresh barkless top,
whose conical shape
if it weren't so high,
one could almost assume it
beaver-gnawed.

On it lichen after lichen:
as if at some distant time of war,
striped, rough-hewn flying saucers
had zipped in with such speed
they embedded half of themselves
in this tough maple's wizened trunk.

Now the warty right arm
of what remains of this
old, diseased warrior
extends upward to press
against its split-off self
as the thinner, longer arm
reaches as if in supplication
toward a narrow opening in the sky.

Transformation
(Rock Lake Trail)

A green, invigorated orchard
of hungry ferns feast
on forest floor enrichment
leeching out the corpse
of a fallen pine

they once were in awe of
as it towered
closer to the sky
than they could
ever imagine.

Aswirl

A wash of water
commences again
to edge itself
out of the rush

of cascading stream,
excavating
its ever enlarging
inlet, flowing

a wavier current
in the widening swirl
of freshet pond
as grain by grain

it shoulders aside
the wood surround
that frames its haven
of light and shade.

Outlier

From somewhere not too far
off the trail the resonant glop glop.

We pause for silence to listen.
We spot him nearer than expected:

In the fine whiskered underbrush
lurks our renegade outlaw:

Hiding out so as not to be
apprehended, while exclaiming

in loud chipmunk-ese,
I am a man among men.

Branchosaurus

With small effort of one of
several limbs it holds off
its lunging stiff-snake attacker,

nor deigns to notice the thin
underbrush in which it plants
its coarse-skinned self. Bark,

trunkish muscles tense,
its pincered head warning
us: Another footfall

and hiking boots will be
emptied of their occupants
and all that they sustain.

Fallen Basswood in Cold October

Under lanky arms
cold blisters of ice
score the trunk's barked

arroyos, filling them
till their dark lacing effaces,
leaving a smooth skin

ornamented by wounds
of luminescent crystal.

Loon Peering

Elegant neck bends:
ripple-less litheness:
arc of dark oval head
into the lake:

Its close-feathered island
floats with sure motion:
crimson eyes peer
into the sheer

clarity of deep waters
clear down to where
fish of a mere several
ounces to heft

much greater, veering
or straight-swimming
are locked
into its hungry
radar antenna.

Prey Pursuit

Loon predator dive scarcely
   wrinkles the sunlit
   surface mirror as
     suddenly

dark angular feet alone
   show like branches
   quickly thrust
     upward by potent

mystery of these waters:
   here and gone
   as the entire body
     beak, head

poised in plunge, wings
   hugged tight,
   legs, feet straight
     as ballerina

on pointe, transforms
   into a focussed
   underwater torpedo
     with its own

brain that orders feet
   rudder-like to
   zig and zag as the fish
     zigs, zags:

Unerringly locked
    on target, a true
    smart living
        missile honing

in until the perch
    is swept bolt-like
    into the falcon-speed
        opened points

of the unerring
    pincer
        beak.

Loons Aloft

A percussive orchestra
of flapping wings
moves the flock
of sharp-beaked,
stretch-necked ovals

under a dimming sky
near the lake's far end,
fanning a primal wind,
part of a strange,
anciently-etched harmony
as momently they slice
across the distant
dusk-green mountain.

A purposeful pair draws me
into the audacity of
a slow dip down,
a bold infringing
of alien country,
braving tremolo warnings
from waters below.

Part way down
they wisely turn and rise,
levelling off, persisting
till near our end of the lake,
comfort zone of home.

Their delight a rush,
downward plowing-through-air!
The male's resonant hoot
announces they are in
the nest's instinctive belonging.

Trying to grasp all
I feel a drawing-in
as if some multi-winged
beast of graced myth
rides on powerful winds
down into the dark
and light of my soul.

Climbing Mount Van Hoevenberg

Hour and a half drive
from Blue Mountain Lake
underlaid with weather doubt.
Chance it we say chance it.

Level trail approach: promising
in spite of soggy ground,
a beaver gated community whose
marshy port of entry seems designed

to keep out non-tenacious intruders.
We thank ourselves for waterproofing
boots onslog onslog spongey
wetlands until the first rise.

Better foot-wise, more secure,
rather rocks and root gnarls than boggy
ambiguity. Pole at the ready,
I follow Nancy up the fairly steep

foothill ascent summit-ward.
Wet snow flaking the trail, more
descending, on with ponchos
we're prepared aren't we. Up and off

to our left a snarled mass of dark blue cloud
threatens storm on the mountain. Stop? Yes.
Turn around? Yes. No. We who hate to even
glance at watches during a climb give ourselves

"about" a quarter hour standing in
semi-hope till the white assaulter
ceases, the dark cloud mass still looming.
Give it a try, poles anchoring us as third legs,

step after step now relief giving us
fresh thirsty eyes to absorb maple, beech,
brightened to mystical yellow by new-emerged
dappled sunlight, a sudden eye-tugging arrayed

splendor kissed by tints of oak-leaf brown,
contrasted conifers whose sturdy
looms speak reassurance of the suddenly friendly
slope whose mission to make us out of breath
seems now a rarely beautiful thing.

Luck: at the summit's reach, clearing skies
crystalize the vista: a vast wisp-like
cushion of smaller red-purple-yellow-sepia-
brown-green cushions as if, had we gigantic arms,
we could reach out, down, feel them
as cottony softness.

These wonders would last
but for the abrupt chill wind clawing
up the other side of the mountain,
sending us--without pausing for sandwiches,
energized by: a strand of licorice,
trickles of water, coffee, and desire--

down over slippery-leaved
slick-rooted–rocked
familiarities
with as much dispatch
as we can manage,
poles punching anchored spots,
balancing three entities:

Need to reach the bottom,
Prudent protection of knees,
The gold-brown splendor
still on the slope abiding.

Rite of Passage

Barely around the curve of shore
smothered by thick morning mist,
in the dark silhouette of bush
small awkward web feet persist

in a presto dashing sprint into
water barely kissed by light.
Uneven flutter of wings, a loud splash:
the young loon's maiden flight.

Code Immemorial

A reddish lavender stretch of horizon
lengthens its light, cushiony pelt,
dissolving at the moment
its deepening screed
seems about to be read,
understood.

Toothed Abyss

The long-broken-off trunk
of the great silver maple
sprawls back, back, lengthy,
massive along the woods floor.

I gape into depth upon depth
of its hollow maw, the massive
splinters of its lips aiming lance-like
at the softness of my human flesh.

My slow concentration imagines
since its break and fall, decades
of lichen-insect enlarging
gaps in its substance.

Faintly audible gnawings:
Tiny maws do their work
on the fetid core as the gaped mouth
glares eyeless at the effrontery
of my stare into its darkness.

Rescue

Around a piney bend
of Rock Lake Trail
the broken upper body
of a beech, its fall halted:
a mid-air shoulder catch
by a stalwart maple's arm
skyward stretched.

The maple, her other arm
also extended upward,
maintains posture erect
though looking surprised
to be cradling this friend
after so many years.

She must know that the frozen
moment will one day unfreeze,
the honorable arm dismember,
carrying its rescued victim
shattering down, down
to the spongy mass that will,
with its rankle of multiple mouths,

slowly soak out
whatever of life lingers
in both stilled limbs,
enlarging all into
a newly vigorous
microbial kingdom.

Sound

Even the stillness
is not still enough
to prepare for
the rise and fall
of the loon's chant.

Three Loons

Dive deep into
   what scent-full
      squiggle-food depths
         remaining down

long enough to
   satisfy, then surface,
      bob their heads
         shedding water,

swim away as if
   they had dined with
      finest ringed napkins,
         cutlery, crystal—

Great Camp aristocrats
   holding erect necks,
      postured heads in
         fearless, sedate dignity.

Surfacing

Without warning
through darkened mirror of water
startlingly emerges
as if from layers of dream
the head of the loon.

Tangled Conundrum

Mass of overturned roots,
squirrly earth its fur,
bedizened by jewels
of multi-sized embedded stones,
one a pale, pupilled eye

glancing askance
from the flattish head
of this squat behemoth

making it seem the shape
of a colossal cynic
as it queries out of its
root-dirt entwinings:

If I who anchored this pine giant,
could by the northern wind god
be thus surprised, terrorized
in thunderous down-topple,

how can you, unanchored one
with no earth balast,
begin to presume
you will not be
thus riven
by a muscled blast
of the same divine raucousness?

A Pause in the Trail

Up Mount Jo
we call a small halt
on the root-and-stone-
trail to indulge
in an eye feast
of reds, oranges,
greens, yellows.

Near enough to touch it
we draw back:
Two massive
dinosaur feet
whose splayed toes
in decor of bright
moss-green, anchor
twin beech giants
into the piney earth.

Mount Jo Rock Face

After a mile and a half
over a hodgepodge
of beech, aspen, maple,
pine roots in all lurking
shapes of ankle-twisting gnarl,

facing a sheer face
of massive grey rock
promising the toughest
clamber yet despite the occasional
merciful erosion gully and crack,

a paradox: Slog-slowed
legs surge awake,
readying us for our final
arm-flexing, finger-scratching,
boot-hold-seeking stretch toward

the just-visible tops
of summit spruces
beckoning us
to share what they witness
illumined by
a welcoming blue sky.

From Mount Jo Summit

A massive shadow spider clings
hard to the upward slope
as if it knows
the wraith of cloud
that births its essence
will in a few moments
wisp itself into air
in the remote distance.

Needled Chamber

Downward we make our way,
glad for sturdy poles, treaded soles
to keep us firm on the wet trail-stones
of the agéd mountain's sloped shoulder.

Unexpectedly, our feet relieve
into needled cushion as we ease
into a copse of conifers
that quietly hail our entry:

A lodgement of memories this,
with its soft mutter of brooklet
water fingering its way over
the old jagged stones. As we

will remember the all of this,
so they remember, will for eons
remember the all of us.

Reciprocity

Spruce roots down-hunker
   in the inches-thick
      compost shell of the mountain.

Some from curiosity
   I brush with my hand. What are
      these curve-edged intruders
         gluing themselves to the roots—

parasites sucking out
   the tree's life? I glance up
      at the scrap of sky
         between conifer summits:

It holds me with its centuries
   eye that empowers my sight
      to see the anomaly:

parasitic lichen shapes
   that moisture-nurture
      an otherwise thirst-famished
         spruce whose bark skin

they in turn welcome
   as it shelters their clinging
      forms from death.

Dismemberments

A few yards off
the unmarked trail
I pick my way
to an enormous cairn
piled like long-weathered bones.

Looking back
the nascent path has become
an indecipherable mangle
of bush and rock.

I make my way up the cairn.
I bend down, closely peer
into its vague striations
that may have once
branched off
a ridge's reliable spine:

Gross mismatchings,
shatter of half-tracings:
remnants of slopes
to an apex of hummock
or sacred mound.

No spirit-powered Hodadenon
or prophet Ezekiel,
I nonetheless begin
to arrange the disparity,
hoping to detect the dim
ancient pattern with which
I could make them coalesce
into their stone eloquence.

Sorriso

Suddenly steeper upward grade
peopled by rebel-defiant rocks
in attention-demanding
angles, shapes,

my pole probing leafy spots
for lurking sharpnesses,
my next step arrested:
Off to the right a massive

roundish stone, its weather-coarsened
skin holding me with the crooked
smile of a primal prophet whose
ever-more-evident silent chuckle

seems to sense faint rag tag
remnant shapes failing to roost
in a far-off wind only its near-lichened
slit of an eye can see.

Prone Spruce

This trunk has not been
long supine. Its barklines
are fresh and strong
as if it were still erect,
well-rooted in the creviced mountain.

This despite two warty masses
of pale lichen, one staring
with famished sockets of eyes,

the other in low swirls
of a pale white gown
caressing into the crust.

Enwound: Theme and Variation

I

There at the turn as I unglue
my eyes from the treacherous
loose-stone trail—muscular
octopus arms embrace
a large grey glacial erratic.

Last century: root limbs stretching
outward from small
moss-lichen nurturance
atop the massive rock's center.

Down over the rock's edges
seeking fingers probed deep
into the leaf-compost skin
of the mountain whose richness
had nurtured all
fortunate competitors---

And there it stands—
the yellow birch whose upward pull
thrust its barked torso more and more
into available sunlight
where now it towers
above them all.

Its six grey calloused arms
hold in tensile strangle/love
the forceful mass
that a century ago
could with the slightest tilt
have nullified all that it is.

II

What at first appears
a strangulation grip,
octopus arms extending
from the base of the barked column

around the massive captive
rock, as if to crush it,
is something else entirely:

The birch tree decades ago
a tough seed on the austere
cuisine atop this stone table,

supplied with just enough
detritus dirt collected
in the just-deep-enough dent
the considerate rock allowed to form,

the grateful birch in turn,
as it made its arduous climb
past competitors to its present
vast height, gratefully holding

its mother foundation
in ever tighter embrace
as its arm-roots sought,
dug into, partook of
the larger mother
on which all reside.

Quintuplets

Sprung from the same portion
of the earth mother's womb
on this high slant stone,
five birch trunks rise

like tall, lithe sisters
celebrating survival and grace
with smiles of diffused sun
on their white, smooth-barked skin,

celebrate togetherness as
a high leaf-flute ensemble
soft but late-autumn audible,
played by the breath of wind
gusting down the shoulder of the mountain.

In the Pines

Just into the pines
not far from shore
the voice quickly rises
rapidly descends
in moments across
the barely wrinkled water.

Forest dirge
pining away
the loon chants
wolf-like,
his song.

At times
with the right wind,
mix of air and water
he seems, though distant,
immense back there
where my hawkeye glasses
cannot penetrate,
ferret out

even the dim outline
of his feral charm,
though sun has a hand-breadth
before it touches
the tops of the conifers
spreads molten
dips down
beyond the mountain.

He calls again
or is it she
from another enclave
answering from
dimness to dimness
out of obscurity?

They both in turn
likely able to clearly see,
quietly wonder
why this sheen-eyed
two-legged creature
stands so still,
frozen, staring
as if to spring.

Squeezing In

The male loon
over a lake
not his own
where strange loons swim
does not sing.

In a house where
I have never been
where the host who invited me
is occupied with food, wine,
I see that all circles
seem to know each other.
I edge toward one.

Two of the ten loons
on the lake below
tremolo a warning.
The stranger continues
to circle, hesitating, ready
to fly elsewhere.

My edging feels awkward,
embarrassing. All chat
amicably, two sip nervously,
with sidelong glances my way.
I stand indecisively.

The other eight loons are silent,
looking up with necks outstretched.
The tremolos cease,
the stranger begins his angled descent,
webbed feet slowing the splashdown,
joining them, observing closely.
Extended necks pull in,
he pulls into the circle,
they circle as the former group
plus one.

I try to catch the eye of someone,
move a little closer
but not within touchable distance.
Neither rejection nor invitation.

The strange loon moves with the others
into a figure eight pattern, proud
elegance of motion.

A man in maroon tie is willing
to notice me, smiles slightly,
nudging to his left to allow me
a small space
to partially enter.

The group of loons
one by one
take shallow dives,
all watching the one diving,
the stranger diving
just like the rest,
observed just like the rest.

The group converses about
a subject I know nothing about
and care even less, but I exude
cordiality nonetheless.
It would be inconsiderate
to edge out, now that I have
made it this far in.

Dives become louder, splashier,
All seem to appreciate the demonstrations.
The stranger knows he is in,
will be allowed to fish on
their territorial waters
for part of this late afternoon.

I attempt to converse,
one or two seem to warm
to me a little, most
obviously preferring
to leave things as they were
while putting on a show
of civility.

After not long a time
the strange loon thrashes
his feet over the water
accelerating into takeoff,
soars for a time, splashes
down not far from shore,
comfortable, at ease,
peers, dives,
comes up with several fish
which he swallows.

After several moments
I edge my way out
with a drink-need excuse
to seek the luck of conversation
at the libation table
in the kitchen.

Adirondac

In memory of Richard Hugo

Within what was a two-hundred-family
village carved by McIntyre and Co
by pluck, planning and strong-willed mind

out of this remote spot near Marcy, now
one can peer through what was a window,
to where she made her simple preparation to dine,

meat, potatoes, bread, maybe a touch
of vegetable, his footfall the same time

or thereabouts every weekday, signal
to set the table, children used to the grime

on his face and hands, ore dust that even
his boots and uniform removed at the mine

could not shield him from. Four or five
of them would have had grace said, a sign

that hunger was about to be appeased,
talk about the kids, him about a line

of ore newly emerged from nondescript rock,
the drilling, pounding through dust to tap the vein

of promised iron, the complicated smelter
process, from such impure lode to refine

until it became malleable, pride that dad
was part of creating structures, a grand design,

a critical segment of the Adirondacks,
New York state itself, this is a fine

thing we do for our country dust or no
he might have said, with maybe a son chiming

in dad we're proud. The wife with weary
nod gathering dishes. None with any suspicion

of just how soon the whole thing would come
to nothing, nor, in its own fourscore time,

resurrect through the marvelous almost divine
grace of that impurity titanium.

Now such pasts flow into one's mind
under, around the roof at crushed incline,
the moss, the ragged holes, the dried grapevine.

Final Things

the last leaf falls
from the stemmed twig
eases itself
off the small branch

cracks away
from the tough limb

worn, wearies
itself with hardly
a sound away
from the main
trunk

thuds, reclines
insect-lichen-moldering
in its heart's fetor faint
revolvings:
detach, disfigure,

transitory delights,
fermenting diurnal hopings
staving off
the transcendent shimmer
of its rebirthing.

Mother and Child

(Hiking up Sawyer Mountain)

As I pause along the conifer-bordered path,
glance up the slope to my right,
two grey glacial erratic boulders
loom on the mountainside
like a downward-swimming child whale
with, behind and to her right,

her massive mother, equally frozen
in mid-thrust of swimming,
staring hard at me with
perplexed, vigilant eyes.

From Sawyer Mountain Summit

A cloud shadow lays its gentle fingers
on the multi-colored cushion of forest,
like a patient bridegroom
moving his hand
up toward the summit face of his bride
who is wearing a wedding gown
of finely-laced sister clouds

trailing along her spine
and ever farther down her body
as if to conceal
from my curious eyes
the mystical marriage-rite
of earth and sky.

The Hedges

In the mid part of a small incline,
the unmistakable sign on Adirondack pine,
turn off the main road into a gentle curve
deeper into the wooded surround,

gently sloping downward to the snug
nestle of old great camp village:
lodges and rooms of massive stone,
of flex-strength conifers: pine, spruce,

hemlock and other sturdy brothers
of all the living trees that snuggle
around this place. These robust
habitations do not feel deprived

by lack of rush or frenzy. Their ample
bellies are filled with the sustenance
of aged, well-used book upon book,
game upon game the same.

Outwards the rim of shoreline
leads the eye across Blue Mountain Lake
to the distant uplift of Castle Rock:
tan-grey eminence in the all-shaded yellow,
red, brown mountain cushion.

Breakfasts, dinners fit for the queens and kings
we feel while here, we are, queens and kings
not of worry-wracked powerful thrones,
but a family of everyone queen and king,

friends with whom these many October turnings
familiarity breeds a fondness deep as the waters
between our shore and the heights beyond.

In late evenings, fireplace smiling
its warm enfolding, we are enfolded
in the cozy space as if in a time-warp soothe
from which we would just as soon never waken.

Mist and darkness cushion our gentle lull
into dream-like waters, to the tremolo, yodel, and wail
of loons distant and far, mystical fountains
of sound calling to each other, calling to us
to snuggle ourselves forever in these mountains.

CPSIA information can be obtained
at www.ICGtesting.com
Printed in the USA
LVIW010219061212

310177LV00002B